# mini EXPLORERS
# Space

**Written by: Kirsty Neale**
**Illustrated by: Gary Joynes**

*igloo*

# The Night Sky

Space is what you see when you look up at the night sky. It's so big, scientists think it might stretch on forever. Space and everything in it is called the **Universe**.

The stars look like tiny dots of light, all about the same distance away, but some are much nearer to us than others.

▶ Our home planet, Earth, is a huge ball of rock. It spins in space, like a basketball spinning on the end of a player's finger!

◀ Shooting stars aren't stars at all – they're lumps of rock known as **meteors**. As they rush towards Earth, they burn brightly in the night sky.

The nearest object to us in space is the Moon. From Earth, it appears to change shape each night. These shapes are known as phases of the Moon.

▲ The **Milky Way galaxy** is made up of billions of stars. We can see part of it as a thick, cloudy-white band in the night sky.

# A Closer Look

Stargazers have been watching the night sky for thousands of years. If you look at space through a **telescope**, everything appears bigger and brighter.

▼ Star atlases and **planispheres** are maps of the night sky that show the positions of the stars.

Large telescopes are kept in a building called an **observatory**.

▲ Telescopes either use a long lens or a curved mirror to form an image, and help you see objects across the Universe.

**The first telescopes were invented**

◀ The dome-shaped roof of an observatory opens up, so the telescope's **lens** can be pointed out into the night sky.

▼ Computers help telescopes to find particular objects in space quickly. They also record information about objects seen.

# The Sun and Other Stars

Stars are enormous balls of fire, burning up a gas called hydrogen. There are over 100 billion stars in the Milky Way galaxy, and millions of other galaxies with even more stars.

▶ Supernovas are huge explosions that happen when large stars run out of gas to burn. Their light is billions of times brighter than the Sun's.

Blue stars are the hottest stars, red are the coolest, and yellow and white stars are medium hot.

After a star explodes, the pieces that are left collapse and suck in light, which can't escape. This is called a black hole.

In ancient times, many people prayed

## Constellations

Some groups of stars seem to make patterns in the sky. The Ancient Greeks named these groups, or **constellations**, after animals and heroes. The stars may not be near each other in space.

The Great Bear

Pegasus

Orion

The Sun is the nearest star to Earth. Burning gas shoots from its surface in flames that stretch for thousands of miles.

to the Sun, believing it was a god.

# Planets

Eight planets circle around the Sun. Together, they are called the Solar System. The four planets nearest the Sun are made of rock. Farther away are four much larger gas and ice planets.

▶ Jupiter spins faster than the other planets. Huge storms, such as the Great Red Spot, form in its gassy clouds.

▶ Saturn's rings are made of billions of pieces of rock and ice whirling around the planet.

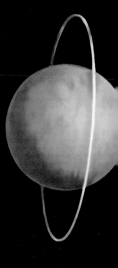

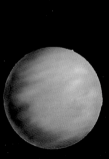

▼ Pluto is no longer described as a planet. It's one of 70,000 icy objects in part of space called the Kuiper Belt.

Uranus

Pluto

Neptune

The biggest mountain in the Solar

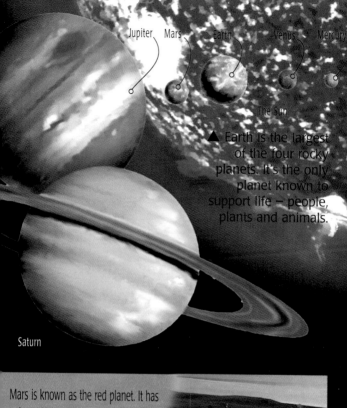

Jupiter  Mars  Earth  Venus  Mercury

The Sun

▲ Earth is the largest of the four rocky planets. It's the only planet known to support life – people, plants and animals.

Saturn

Mars is known as the red planet. It has volcanoes, canyons and valleys, but no rivers or seas. In 2008, a spacecraft named the Phoenix Mars Lander discovered water ice on Mars.

# Race to the Moon

Moons spin around planets. They always follow the same path, called an **orbit**. In the 1960s, the United States and the Soviet Union raced to land a man on Earth's only moon.

helmet

primary life support system / air tank

display and control module

gloves

◀ Neil Armstrong was the first person to walk on the Moon. His spacesuit held radios, tools and an air tank, so he could breathe.

boots

So far, only 12 people have ever se

America won the space race in July 1969, when a huge **rocket**, Saturn V, carried the Apollo 11 spacecraft into space.

The Apollo 11 spacecraft was made in three sections. Only one of these, the four-legged **Lunar Module**, actually landed on the Moon.

As the Moon orbits Earth, we see sunlight reflecting off different amounts of the Moon's surface.

There is no wind or rain on the Moon, so the footprints left by the **astronauts** will last for thousands of years.

foot on the surface of the Moon.

# Asteroids and Comets

Our Solar System contains thousands of pieces of rock, called **asteroids**, all moving around the Sun. Some are as small as a bus, while others are the size of a small planet.

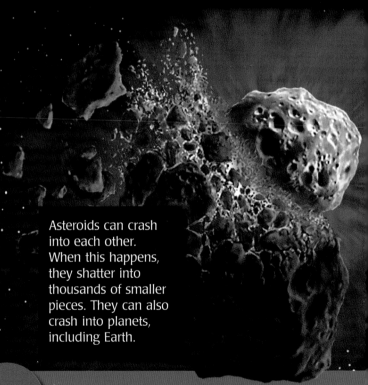

Asteroids can crash into each other. When this happens, they shatter into thousands of smaller pieces. They can also crash into planets, including Earth.

Thanks to solar winds, the tail of a

▼ The largest asteroid in the Solar System is named Ceres. It's about 620 miles (1,000 km) wide and is described as a dwarf planet.

▲ A comet is a huge ball of frozen rock, dust and gas, with a fiery tail that can be millions of miles long.

▼ The **asteroid belt** is between Mars and Jupiter.

comet always points away from the Sun.

# Exploring Space

Ever since man landed on the Moon, we've dreamed of exploring the rest of the Solar System. **Unmanned** space **probes** have photographed each of the eight planets and gathered all kinds of useful information.

▶ The Hubble Space Telescope has taken some amazing photographs, including pictures of stars being born.

Soviet **cosmonaut** Uri Gagarin was the first human sent into space. He orbited Earth in a tiny spacecraft named Vostok 1.

The first animal in space was a dog named Laika. In 1957 she was launched into orbit on board a Soviet spacecraft.

The probe Voyager 1 has left the

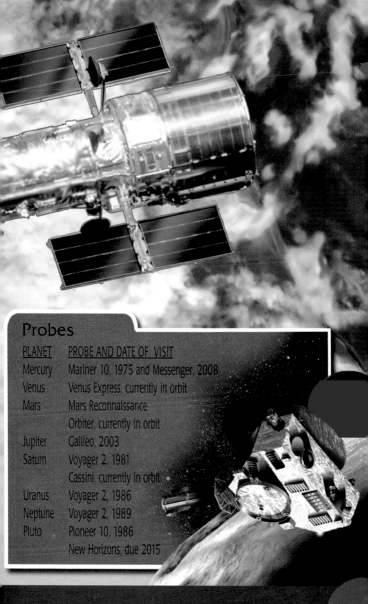

## Probes

| PLANET | PROBE AND DATE OF VISIT |
|---|---|
| Mercury | Mariner 10, 1975 and Messenger, 2008 |
| Venus | Venus Express, currently in orbit |
| Mars | Mars Reconnaissance Orbiter, currently in orbit |
| Jupiter | Galileo, 2003 |
| Saturn | Voyager 2, 1981 |
| | Cassini, currently in orbit |
| Uranus | Voyager 2, 1986 |
| Neptune | Voyager 2, 1989 |
| Pluto | Pioneer 10, 1986 |
| | New Horizons, due 2015 |

# Space Shuttles

After launching a spacecraft, most rockets fall back to Earth and land in the sea. The Space Shuttle is different. It's designed to land on a runway, so it can be used again.

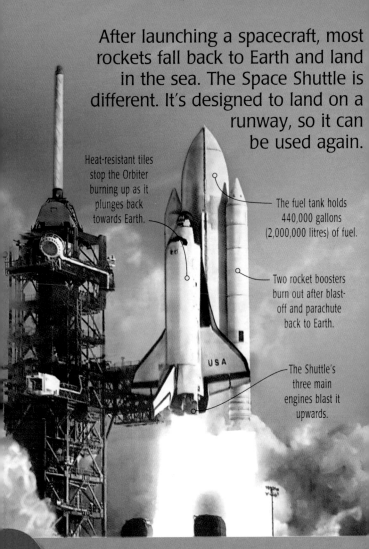

Heat-resistant tiles stop the Orbiter burning up as it plunges back towards Earth.

The fuel tank holds 440,000 gallons (2,000,000 litres) of fuel.

Two rocket boosters burn out after blast-off and parachute back to Earth.

The Shuttle's three main engines blast it upwards.

USA

As it nears Earth, the outside of o

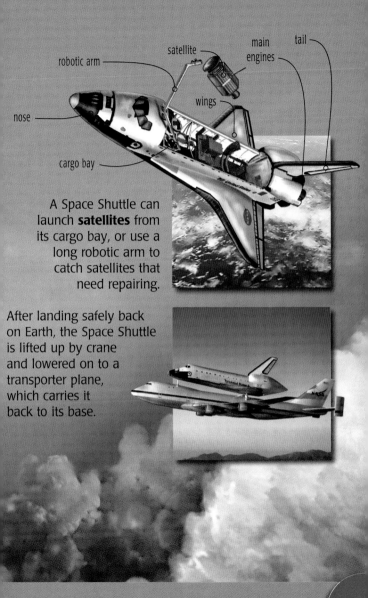

robotic arm

satellite

main engines

tail

nose

wings

cargo bay

A Space Shuttle can launch **satellites** from its cargo bay, or use a long robotic arm to catch satellites that need repairing.

After landing safely back on Earth, the Space Shuttle is lifted up by crane and lowered on to a transporter plane, which carries it back to its base.

**Shuttle heats up to 1,500°C (2,732°F).**

# Space Stations

Astronauts can live on a space station for many months at a time. While there, they carry out scientific experiments and research. Space Shuttles transport astronauts to and from the space station.

▶ The International Space Station (ISS) was built in stages by the United States, Russia, Japan, Canada, Brazil and eleven European countries.

## Weightlessness

Astronauts in space have no weight, and appear to float through the air. At night, they strap themselves into sleeping bags, so they don't float away and bump into things!

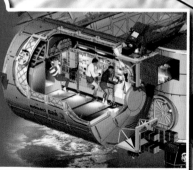

Up in space, the ISS whizzes around,

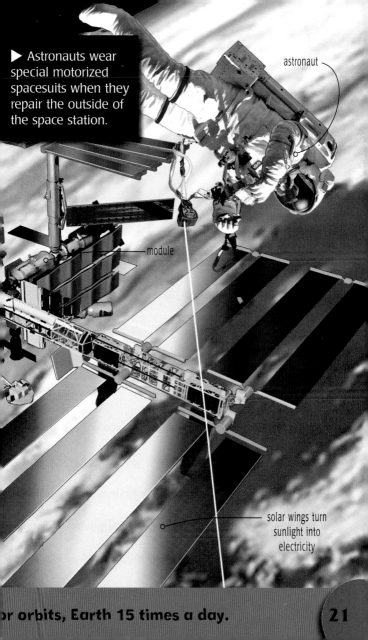

▶ Astronauts wear special motorized spacesuits when they repair the outside of the space station.

astronaut

module

solar wings turn sunlight into electricity

# Glossary

**Asteroids**
Rocky objects, widely ranging in size, that orbit the Sun.

**Asteroid belt**
Part of the Solar System between Mars and Jupiter that is packed with asteroids.

**Astronauts**
People trained to go into space.

**Constellation**
A group of stars seen from Earth that appear to form a pattern.

**Cosmonaut**
A Russian, or Soviet, astronaut.

**Galaxy**
A very large group of stars.

**Lens**
A curved piece of glass that makes objects look closer to us.

**Lunar**
Relating to the Moon.

**Meteor**
A piece of rock that creates a bright streak of light as it falls through the Earth's atmosphere.

**Milky Way**
Our home galaxy.

**Module**
Part of a spacecraft that can be separated from the rest and used on its own.

**Observatory**
A building from which people can view the night sky, usually through a large telescope.

**Orbit**
The curved path around a planet or star that an object in space follows.

**Planisphere**
A type of circular star chart.

**Probes**
Small spacecraft with no-one on board, usually carrying scientific equipment and cameras.

**Rocket**
A tube-shaped object that moves very quickly by forcing out burning gas.

**Satellites**
Small objects sent up into space and used for gathering or sending out information.

**Telescope**
An instrument that makes far-away objects look larger and closer, using lenses or mirrors.

**Universe**
Everything in space, the whole of space.

**Unmanned**
A spacecraft that has no people on board to operate it or control its course.